Your Amazing Body

Nose

by Imogen Kingsley

Bullfrog Books

Ideas for Parents and Teachers

Bullfrog Books let children practice reading informational text at the earliest reading levels. Repetition, familiar words, and photo labels support early readers.

Before Reading
- Discuss the cover photo. What does it tell them?
- Look at the picture glossary together. Read and discuss the words.

Read the Book
- "Walk" through the book and look at the photos. Let the child ask questions. Point out the photo labels.
- Read the book to the child, or have him or her read independently.

After Reading
- Prompt the child to think more. Ask: What scents do you enjoy smelling? Which scents do you most dislike?

Bullfrog Books are published by Jump!
5357 Penn Avenue South
Minneapolis, MN 55419
www.jumplibrary.com

Copyright © 2018 Jump! International copyright reserved in all countries. No part of this book may be reproduced in any form without written permission from the publisher.

Library of Congress Cataloging-in-Publication Data

Names: Kingsley, Imogen, author.
Title: Nose / by Imogen Kingsley.
Description: Minneapolis, MN: Jump!, Inc., 2017.
Series: Your amazing body
Audience: Ages 5–8. | Audience: K to grade 3.
Includes bibliographical references and index.
Identifiers: LCCN 2016051869 (print)
LCCN 2016052894 (ebook)
ISBN 9781620316887 (hardcover: alk. paper)
ISBN 9781620317419 (pbk.)
ISBN 9781624965654 (ebook)
Subjects: LCSH: Nose—Juvenile literature.
Smell—Juvenile literature.
Anatomy—Juvenile literature.
Senses and sensation—Juvenile literature.
Classification: LCC QM505 .K534 2017 (print)
LCC QM505 (ebook) | DDC 612.8/6—dc23
LC record available at https://lccn.loc.gov/2016051869

Editor: Jenny Fretland VanVoorst
Book Designer: Molly Ballanger
Photo Researcher: Molly Ballanger

Photo Credits: Dreamstime: Petr Zamecnik, 8–9. Shutterstock: Oksana Kuzmina, 1; Kdshutterman, 3; eurobanks, 4, 5; risteski goce, 4, 5; karamysh, 6–7; Only background, 6–7; Vinicius Tupinamba, 6–7; Delpixel, 10; Happy Together, 11; Yulyazolotko, 12–13; Studio1One, 14–15; ben bryant, 16–17; Thaweewong Vichaiuroroj, 16–17; K13 ART, 18; Neamov, 18; Nolte Laurens, 18, 19; motorolka, 19; wong sze yuen, 20–21; Alila Medical Media, 22; 3Dalia, 23tr; Alex Mit, 23tl; Vinitchavat, 23bl; pathdoc, 24.

Printed in the United States of America at Corporate Graphics in North Mankato, Minnesota.

Table of Contents

Sniff It!	4
Parts of the Nose	22
Picture Glossary	23
Index	24
To Learn More	24

Sniff It!

Meg sniffs.

What does she smell?

Jed smells smoke.
Oh, no!
There is a fire.
He calls 911.

Jo runs up a hill.

Whew!

She breathes in and out.

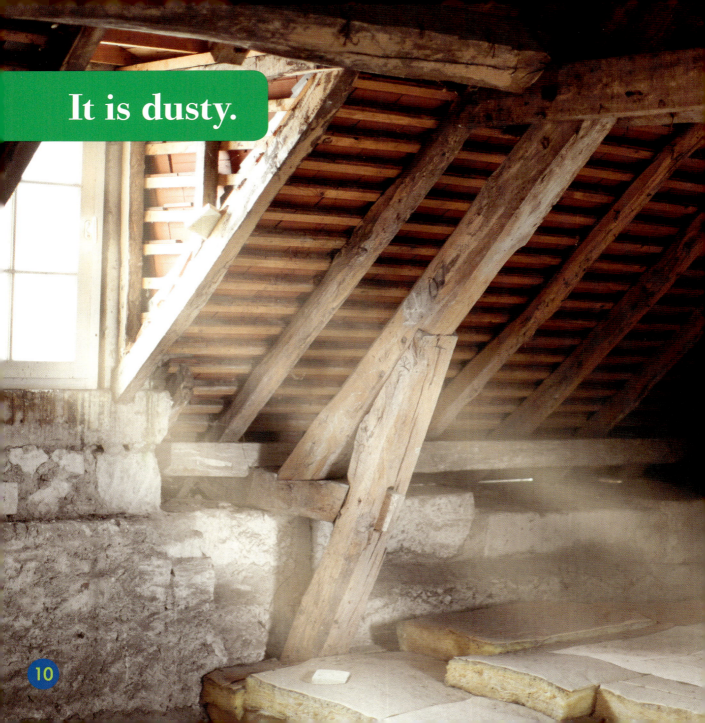
It is dusty.

Ben sneezes. Achoo!
His nose gets rid of the dust.

Your nose is amazing! How does it work?

You have two nostrils.
They take in air.
They let out air.

Your nose has mucus.
It has hairs.
They catch dirt.
They catch germs.

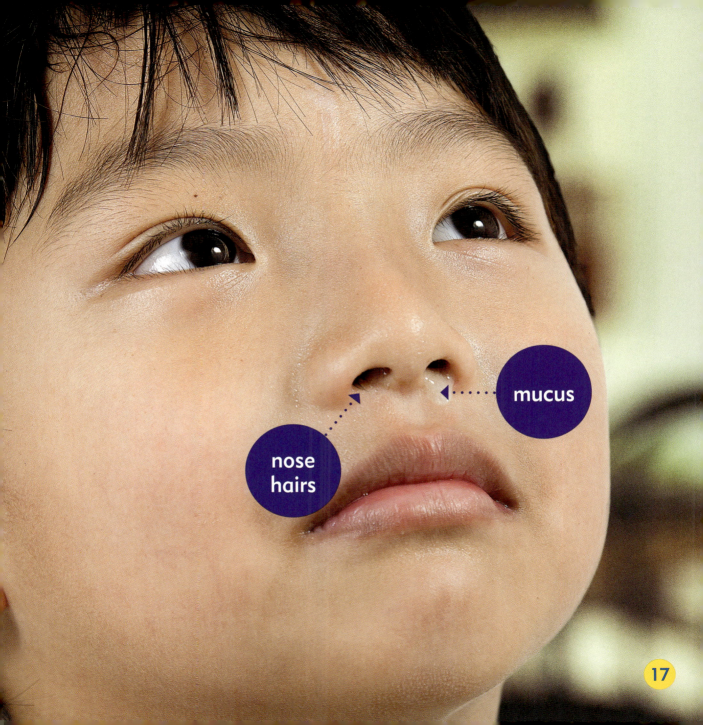

Your nose has scent collectors.

They send a message to your brain.

Your brain tells you what you smell.

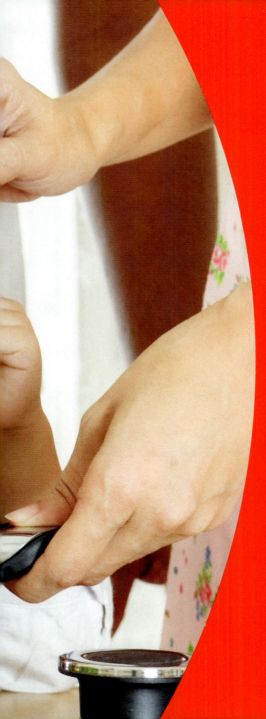

Close your eyes.

Sniff.

What do you smell?

Parts of the Nose

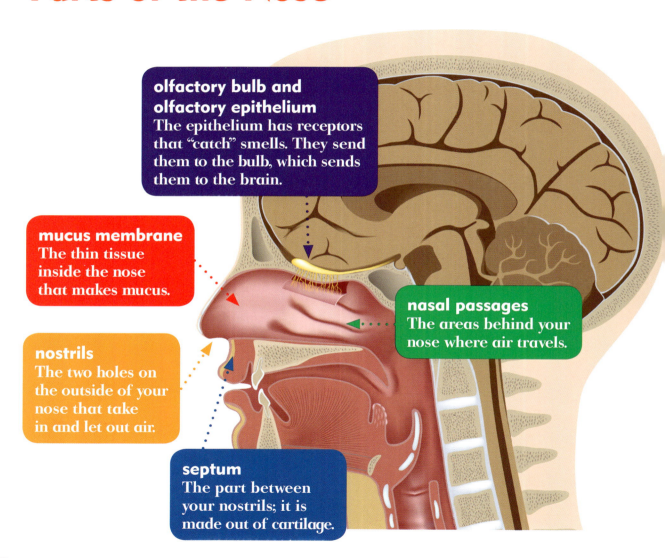

olfactory bulb and olfactory epithelium
The epithelium has receptors that "catch" smells. They send them to the bulb, which sends them to the brain.

mucus membrane
The thin tissue inside the nose that makes mucus.

nasal passages
The areas behind your nose where air travels.

nostrils
The two holes on the outside of your nose that take in and let out air.

septum
The part between your nostrils; it is made out of cartilage.

Picture Glossary

brain
The "message center" part of your body.

germ
A very small living thing that can make you sick.

dust
Very fine powder that builds up on the surface of things, like furniture.

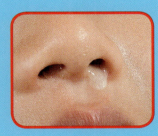
mucus
A thick liquid that is made by the body; when it combines with dirt and germs, it makes boogers.

Index

air 15
brain 18, 19
breathes 8
dirt 16
germs 16
hairs 16
mucus 16
nostrils 15
smell 4, 7, 19, 21
smoke 7
sneezes 11
sniff 4, 21

To Learn More

Learning more is as easy as 1, 2, 3.

1) Go to www.factsurfer.com

2) Enter "nose" into the search box.

3) Click the "Surf" button to see a list of websites.

With factsurfer.com, finding more information is just a click away.